LEASED AND LOST UPDATE:
THE ECONOMIC AND ENVIRONMENTAL IMPACT OF THE REPEAL OF SECTION 3 OF THE FEDERAL COAL LEASING AMENDMENTS ACT OF 1976

by

James S. Cannon

Edited by

Alice Tepper Marlin

and

Paula Lippin

A COUNCIL ON ECONOMIC PRIORITIES PUBLICATION

ISBN: 87871-050-7

85-10,556

Council on Economic Priorities
30 Irving Place, New York, NY 10003
212/420-1133

Printed in the United States of America

BIOGRAPHY

James Cannon is a researcher, author, and consultant on energy development, the environment, and related public policy issues. He has held positions as research associate and consultant to several non-profit organizations and government agencies. He is currently a Program Associate at Western Network in Santa Fe, New Mexico.

Mr. Cannon has written a number of books, articles, and reports that examine environmental and energy issues related to western natural resource development, the federal coal leasing program, the direct use of coal for power generation, the research and development of innovative energy technologies, and the structure of the U.S. coal industry.

PREFACE

The Council on Economic Priorities published *Leased and Lost* in May, 1974. *Leased and Lost* was the first independent analysis of the federal coal leasing program to disclose the near giveaway of western public coal lands to private industry without regard to environmental or land use planning considerations. At that time coal was being mined on only a small fraction of leased acreage. Speculators held many leases in the hope of profitting from their future resale to bona fide developers.

Congress responded through the Federal Coal Leasing Amendments Act of 1976 (FCLAA) to prevent public land speculation and to tighten environmental protection standards. Section 3, the subject of this report, is one provision in that law. It addresses specifically the leases issued before 1970 by limiting the rights of leaseholders to hold non-producing leases. The legislative history of FCLAA is replete with references to the CEP study to justify many of the reforms created in the law.

Eight years after FCLAA was enacted, Congress is faced with a vigorous lobbying effort to repeal or modify Section 3, spearheaded by energy companies and their trade organizations. This study is CEP's attempt to contribute constructively to the current Section 3 debate by updating the key findings of *Leased and Lost* with regard to lease speculation. We hope that the new information the report provides will improve the prospects for the sound management of the nation's public coal lands.

The report has been researched and written by James Cannon, the author of CEP's *Leased and Lost*, a decade ago. He is currently working as a Program Associate at Western Network in Santa Fe. Western Network maintains a computerized database of information about each of the more than 600 existing federal coal leases. That database provided the information used by Mr. Cannon to complete the analysis performed for CEP and presented in this report.

TABLE OF CONTENTS

SUMMARY

Section 3 is a provision of the Federal Coal Leasing Amendments Act of 1976 (FCLAA) added by Congress largely to discourage speculation with western public coal lands and to propel coal production from leased public land. It was intended to affect primarily the owners of about 500 coal leases issued prior to enactment of FCLAA; over 80 per cent of those lease tracts, which covered more than 16 billion tons of recoverable coal reserves, were not included in active mining operations in 1976.

The sanction provided in Section 3 prohibits any company from obtaining additional public land leases for any mineral covered by the Mineral Leasing Act — including on-shore oil and gas reserves as well as coal — if it had been holding a coal lease for at least ten years without producing coal from the land included in the lease. Thus, two criteria must be met to trigger the sanction: ownership for at least ten years and non-production of coal. The sanction can be avoided if commercial production of coal is achieved, if ownership of non-producing leases is transfered to another company at which time the 10 year "clock" is restarted, or if non-producing leases are relinquished to the government. For pre-FCLAA leases, the sanctions begin to take hold on August 4, 1986, or ten years after enactment of FCLAA.

Consequently, the provision has become the target of a major lobbying effort calling for its repeal or modification. Repeal legislation was debated in both the 97th and 98th Congresses. Although no congressional action was taken, several bills to repeal or amend Section 3 await action by the 99th Congress. Most companies and trade organizations active in the coal business have favored repeal of Section 3. Many national environmental organizations and many western citizen groups favor its enforcement.

Among the many arguments used to support repeal of Section 3 are the following:

- Speculation with public coal lands is no longer a significant problem requiring this legislated "solution";
- Section 3 will disrupt western coal markets by causing either over-production or a coal shortage;
- It will inhibit competition and development of other critical western resources including oil and gas;
- It will reduce leasing revenues to the federal and state governments that share such income;
- Ten years is too short a timetable within which to bring a mine into production; and
- The provision is a punitive act that unjustly hurts pre-FCLAA lessees.

Some key arguments in support of enforcement of Section 3 are:

- It offers an important backstop against continued or renewed speculation;
- Its repeal would provide a financial windfall to a number of

large companies, including several major oil companies;

- It coerces the Department of Interior to enforce diligent development provisions contained, but undefined, in pre-FCLAA leases;
- The provision helps to correct a bias in favor of pre-FCLAA lessees and against post-FCLAA lessees;
- It could help protect the environment by forcing relinquishment of leases in some environmentally-sensitive regions; and
- It will help improve the land use planning and leasing programs of the Department of Interior.

Interest groups in favor of repeal and enforcement of Section 3 cite studies that to date suggest that a large number of leases — up to 70 per cent — and that most of the current coal lessees — up to 80 per cent — could be affected by Section 3 in 1986.

Using an original methodology, this study presents a new analysis of the likely effect of Section 3 on federal coal leases and lessees in 1986. It is the first study to analyze the likely effects of ownership changes, as well as coal mine development status, on the susceptibility of lessees to Section 3 in 1986. The principal findings include the following:

- Studies to date have overstated the number of leases and lessees likely to face Section 3 sanctions in 1986. The owners of only 117 lease tracts, covering 19 per cent of acreage contained in the 500 pre-FCLAA leases, were determined in this study to be likely candidates for Section 3 sanctions beginning in 1986. They include less than one-third of all lessees now owning leases.
- Nearly two-thirds of all pre-FCLAA leases have had some significant ownership change since 1976 that may have a bearing on susceptibility of lessees to Section 3 sanctions in 1986. The owners of 147 leases appear to be exempt from Section 3 sanctions in 1986 by virtue of 117 lease ownership changes (or assignments) that occurred between 1976 and the end of 1984. Leases affected by ownership changes likely to exempt their lessees from Section 3 sanctions in 1986 are almost equal to the leases likely to meet the commercial production requirement.
- The majority of lease tracts, 275, covering 56 per cent of the acreage in pre-FCLAA leases are either likely to be in production by 1986 or have been affected by an ownership change likely to exempt their lessees from Section 3 sanctions in 1986.
- Uncertainty undermines any analysis of Section 3 because a variety of ownership changes since 1976 have unclear implications for the susceptibility of many lessees to Section 3 in 1986. One quarter of pre-FCLAA lease acreage is included in 108 leases. The lessees of this acreage face uncertain prospects of incurring the Section 3 sanctions in 1986. The prinicipal causes of uncertainty are ownership changes affecting 102 leases involving less than 100 per cent assign-

ment of leases among unaffiliated parties. Five types of business transactions were identified (e.g. acquisition of a leaseholding company by another company) that could exempt lessees from Section 3 sanctions in 1986 depending on the legal interpretation assigned to those ownership changes.

- Ownership changes provide a frequently travelled avenue by which lessees avoid the Section 3 sanctions in 1986. Availability and use of this option, which cannot be used by the owners of post-FCLAA leases, undercuts arguments that Section 3 is punitive. To the contrary, by establishing a 10-year deadline, the provision places pre-FCLAA lessees on close to an equal footing with the holders of post-FCLAA leases that must achieve commercial production within 10 years of lease issuance in order to avoid lease cancellation.

- Only 6 per cent of the acreage in pre-FCLAA leases is controlled by unincorporated individuals. Most are assumed to be speculators. Ninety-three percent of that acreage, however, is in leases of which the owners are likely to face Section 3 sanctions in 1986. Thus, some degree of lease speculation by individuals exists and most of those lessees are likely to face Section 3 sanctions in 1986. These facts support the logic behind retaining Section 3. On the other hand, unless the individuals holding non-producing pre-FCLAA leases wish to bid for other leases under the Mineral Leasing Act, they have no reason to fear the Section 3 sanctions.

- Repeal of Section 3 is unlikely to provide a major windfall to oil and gas companies. Only one percent of the acreage controlled by major oil companies and four percent of the acreage controlled by large natural gas companies is likely to fail to meet either the development or ownership criteria for lessees to avoid Section 3 sanctions in 1986.

- Two groups most likely to be seriously affected by enforcement of Section 3 are the steel industry and electric utilities. Seventy-one percent of the acreage controlled by steel companies and 40 percent of the acreage controlled by utilities are likely to fail to meet either the ownership or the development criteria. These industries are not major competitors for other mineral leases. Thus, enforcement of Section 3 is unlikely to have a major effect on competition or development of other western minerals.

- Few leases likely to face Section 3 sanctions beginning in 1986 are located in the four major coal producing regions. In 1983, these regions accounted for over 80 percent of western public land coal production. This suggests that enforcement of Section 3 will not cause large disruption in the major western coal supply markets. It could, however, affect regions now producing small quantities of coal.

- Southwest Utah is the western region with the heaviest concentration of leases unlikely to meet development or ownership criteria to free its lessees from the Section 3 sanctions. Coal development in this region has been vigorously opposed for decades by environmental and conservation organizations who fear development will irreparably harm the fragile desert environment of this area and degrade the environmental values of the many national parks, forests, and monuments located there. This finding offers support for the argument that enforcement of Section 3 will achieve environmental protection objectives.

- If leases are relinquished as a result of enforcement of Section 3, federal and state governments will lose the rental income they produce. In 1983, however, rental income provided less than two percent of all revenue generated from coal leases. Bonus bids from new lease sales and royalties — especially from leases containing the higher royalty rates required by FCLAA — contribute most of the income. If just a few leases relinquished because of Section 3 were re-issued or if other leases were issued in their place, it is likely that the total revenue flow to federal and state governments would be much greater than if pre-FCLAA leases were not relinquished.

- The average date of acquisition of a lease that is likely to fail the development and ownership criteria and leave its owner subject to Section 3 beginning in 1986 was found to be July 7, 1960. The average date of acquisition of those leases by their current owner was December 20, 1966, or just less than 20 years before the Section 3 sanctions take hold in 1986. Thus, most lessees facing Section 3 sanctions have held their leases far longer than the 10-year production deadline set up by the provision — certainly ample time to develop mining operations.

The data in this study suggest that the stakes involved in either the repeal or the enforcement of Section 3 are not nearly as high as most of the interest groups lobbying on the issue argue. Either repeal or enforcement is unlikely to engender apocalyptic consequences. The issues raised in the Section 3 debate are not insignificant, however. They can and should be resolved. The prospects for resolution are likely to be increased if the actual effects of Section 3 are placed in a proper and less dramatic perspective.

The weight of the evidence collected in this study tends to provide greater support for the arguments in favor of Section 3. It is apparent, however, that some of the arguments on both sides have considerable merit. This analysis suggests that Section 3 issues should be re-examined and prioritized in light of the likely effects of Section 3 based on evidence at hand, rather than on theory alone. That re-examination could lead to identification of currently undetected policy options acceptable to all sides. Moreover, it could reveal to Congress a course of action that best serves the public interest instead of actions designed to protect one company or interest group.

The uncertainties surrounding the implications of a number of ownership changes affecting 25 per cent of all acreage included in pre-FCLAA leases will undermine any attempt to re-examine Section 3 issues accurately. Those uncertainties must be resolved by establishing a clear and legally defensible policy by Congress and the Department of Interior.

Until then, assessments of the effects of Section 3 will continue to lack the precision needed to form the basis of sound decision-making.

Although this study generally supports pro-enforcement arguments, implementation of Section 3 as it now stands is likely to entail problems. Some of these problems might best be avoided through amendments to the provision. One example might be an additional sanction requiring advance royalty payments by holders of non-producing pre-FCLAA leases. This could provide an economic disincentive for some speculators to acquire or retain ownership of pre-FCLAA leases. Also, implementation of Section 3 could have especially adverse and unrelated economic effects on companies or industries. A case-by-base review of Section 3 effects on individual companies and industries might identify instances where some relief from the consequences of Section 3 might be justified.

INTRODUCTION

> The Secretary shall not issue a lease or leases under the terms of this Chapter to any person, association, corporation, or any subsidiary, affiliate, or persons controlled by or under common control with such person, association, or corporation, where any such entity holds a lease or leases issued by the United States to coal deposits and has held such lease or leases for a period of ten years when such entity is not, except as provided for in section 207(b) of this title, producing coal from the lease deposits in commercial quantities. In computing the ten-year period referred to in the preceding sentence, periods of time prior to August 4, 1976, shall not be counted. (30 U.S.C. 201(a)(2)(A))

Those 115 words comprise, in full, Section 3 of FCLAA, the Federal Coal Leasing Amendments Act of 1976. Section 3 was enacted by Congress over Presidential veto on August 4, 1976 as part of a comprehensive reform law to overhaul the statutory requirements of the Federal coal leasing program first established under the Mineral Leasing Act of 1920. Section 3 has recently become the target of intensive scrutiny by a number of interest groups and the subject of a sometimes emotional and always highly charged debate over the appropriateness of the limitations it places on the holders of Federal coal leases. Many industry trade organizations and mining companies, with the support of the Department of Interior, now vigorously lobby for the repeal of Section 3. Most conservation and environmental organizations, with the support of many western citizens groups, argue, with equal zeal, for the broadest enforcement of Section 3 permitted by the statute.

At the heart of Section 3 is the prohibition it places on certain companies from obtaining new federal public land leases for any natural resource — including, coal, on-shore oil and natural gas, and several other substances — regulated under the Mineral Leasing Act of 1920. That sanction applies to any company owning a federal coal lease for at least 10 years without producing commercial quantities of coal from the land it covers. The leasing proscription can be removed only when commercial coal production begins or if the company relinquishes its non-producing leases back to the government or sells them to other companies.

The principal purpose of this report is to examine the implications of the enforcement or repeal of Section 3 of the Federal coal leasing program beginning on August 4, 1986, the date the sanctions contained in the provision begin to take effect. Using a unique methodology, the report assesses the number, acreage, location, and ownership of Federal coal leases likely to be subject to the Section 3 sanctions in 1986; those leases and lessees likely to be immune from Section 3; and those leases and lessees that may or may not be affected by Section 3 depending on the interpretation of the language in the law and the resolution of uncertainities surrounding some coal development plans. The data are then studied with respect to their relevance to the major arguments in favor of and opposed to repeal of Section 3. The report concludes by identifying policy considerations Congress may wish to address as it develops and examines new proposals to repeal or modify Section 3.

BACKGROUND OF SECTION 3

From 1920 to 1970 the U.S. Department of Interior managed a leasing program for coal-bearing public lands, located mostly in the western United States. Through this program some 525 leases covering 740,000 acres of land and 16 billion tons of coal were awarded to private industry or individuals. About 20 per cent of western public coal lands are estimated to have been leased between 1920 and 1970. Nearly half of the leases were awarded noncompetitively and without receipt of payment on the part of the lessee. Competition for most of the leases offered at competitive lease sales had been sparse or nonexistent and income from those sales had been insignificant. None of the leased lands had passed through land use planning processes to ascertain suitability for coal development prior to leasing. Provisions of leases included low royalty and rental payments by lessees and contained few requirements for the timely mining of leased coal resources or to ensure land reclamation after mining.

A rapid increase in leasing during the 1960s nearly tripled the number of leases in a ten-year period. Leasing came to a sudden halt in 1971, however, when the Department of Interior (DOI) instituted a moratorium on new leasing pending the completion of a review of the program by the Department. During the next few years, a number of concerns over allegedly inadequate leasing practices were voiced by a variety of interest groups and leasing analysts. As a result, the U.S. Congress began molding legislation to amend the statutes contained in the Mineral Leasing Act governing coal leasing.

Critics of the leasing program raised a number of objections to pre-1970 leasing practices, but none raised public outcry as much as charges of public land speculation on the part of coal lessees. Central to the speculation argument was the fact that only a handful — less than 10 per cent in 1970 — of coal leases covered land on which coal mining was actually taking place. Of a total 16 billion tons of leased reserves, only 7.3 million tons were mined in 1970. Nevertheless, many companies, including small landholders that did not have the financial or technical capability of opening a coal mine, continued to press the Department of Interior to issue more public land coal leases.

Congress addressed the speculation issue and a number of other concerns by creating a patchwork of new statutory requirements for coal leasing in FCLAA. Acreage limitations were placed on the amount of land that could be leased to one company; a "diligent" development provision was enacted requiring coal be mined on all new leases within ten years of their issuance; minimium royalties were raised, pre-lease land use planning and various environmental protection procedures were established; and the Department of Justice was instructed to oversee leasing to ensure that antitrust violations did not occur.

With one exception, the reforms enacted in FCLAA apply to leases issued after passage of the Act and potentially to pre-FCLAA leases only after the first date their lease terms first become due for readjustment — an event that occurs every twentieth anniversary of the date of lease issuance. For example, the higher royalty requirements and other requirements set by FCLAA do not begin to apply to a lease issued in 1970 until 1990.

The one exception is Section 3. In it, Congress attempted to create a disincentive to continued speculation with pre-FCLAA leases by forcing lessees either to produce coal by 1986, to sell non-producing leases, or to relinquish the leases. The peculiar language of Section 3, when compared to the straightforward provisions for post-FCLAA leases reflects, in part, the legal difficulties of applying new laws to existing government contracts. Representative Patsy Mink (D-Hawaii), a sponsor of the House bill that ultimately became FCLAA, referred to such potential problems in the House floor debate over the bill when she said:

> Nor do we wish to trigger sticky constitutional questions involving the taking of legislatively conferred rights by reacting to the deficiencies of the current law with retroactive application of tough new lease standards and terms to lessees who legally gained their rights relying on the provisions of the current law.

Thus, Section 3, unlike the 10 year diligent development provision applying to post-FCLAA leases, does not terminate non-producing pre-FCLAA leases. The leases themselves continue; the sanction applies to lessees and prohibits them only from obtaining any new leases as long as they hold and have held for at least 10 years non-producing coal leases. Also, Section 3 offers pre-FCLAA lessees an option other than producing coal or relinquishing leases to escape the Section 3 sanction. The lessees can sell non-producing leases through a process called lease assignment. This restarts the Section 3 clock for the new lessee.

Congress attempted to pressure the owners of the 90 per cent of existing federal coal leases that were not included in producing coal mines into developing, selling, or forfeiting them through Section 3. The provision also required the Department of Interior for the first time to enforce diligent development standards on pre-FCLAA lessees, a step the agency had been reluctant to take of its own initiative. The sanction appears to have been crafted in the hopes of avoiding constitutional "taking" issues, while being strong enough to correct, at least partially, what a majority within Congress believed a troublesome pattern of speculation with existing public coal land leases.

THE REPEAL MOVEMENT

Implications of Section 3 on the coal leasing program drew little attention during the first five years after passage of FCLAA. The Department of Interior under the Carter administration was busy developing its Federal Coal Management Program, unveiled in mid-1979. This outlined a new leasing program to implement the provisions of FCLAA. The moratorium on new leasing was finally lifted in January, 1981, and shortly thereafter the DOI, under the Reagan Administration, substantially rewrote the leasing regulations and guidelines to the liking of that Adminstration. This touched off a public outcry that eventually resulted in the imposition of another leasing moratorium and the initiation of a series of "blue ribbon" investigations of the leasing program.

During the past three years, Congress has become increasingly drawn into an escalating debate over Section 3. As the deadline for the imposition of the Section 3 sanctions — August 4, 1986 or ten years after enactment of FCLAA — draws nearer, some lessees of pre-FCLAA leases and several industry trade organizations have increased their lobbying efforts to repeal Section 3.

Repeal bills were sponsored in both the 97th Congress — H.R. 5895 introduced by Rep. Ray Kogovsek (D-Colo) and S. 2704 introduced by Sen. Frank Murkowski (R-Alaska) — and in the 98th Congress — H.R. 1530 again introduced by Kogovsek and S. 1634 introduced by Sen. Malcolm Wallop (R-Wyoming). Subcommittee hearing were held on each of the bills; by the Subcommittee on Energy and Mineral Resources of the Committee on Energy and Natural Resources in the case of the Senate bills and the Subcommittee on Mines and Mining (renamed the Subcommittee on Mining, Forest Management, and the Bonneville Power Administration by the 98th Congress) of the Committee on Interior and Insular Affairs in the case of the House bills.

Companies and organizations that have testified in favor of the repeal of Section 3 include, among others, the National Coal Association, the American Mining Congress, The American Petroleum Institute, Consolidation Coal Co., Mobil Oil Corp., Coastal States Energy Co., Utah International Inc., and Pittsburg and Midway Coal Mining Co. Organizations testifying against the repeal of Section 3 have included the National Wildlife Federation, the Western Organization of Resource Councils, the Friends of the Earth, and the Sierra Club.

Although groups standing for and against repeal of Section 3 obviously disagree, both positions maintain that the stakes posed by either abandonment or enforcement of Section 3 are high. Indeed, the issue is emerging as something of a cause celebre for many organizations, and each side has its own apocalypse scenario to describe alleged farreaching implications if their point of view is not adopted. The following portion of the testimony by the President of Pittsburg and Midway Coal Co. before the Senate Subcommittee on Energy and Mineral Resources captures some of the fervor propelling the Section 3 debate.

(F)ailure to repeal Section 3 would have not just . . . long-term local impact that is on the basic structure of the coal industry in the West, but more importantly failure to repeal Section 3 would have strongly adverse national impact in the form of reduced competition, higher coal costs nationwide, and higher energy costs. In addition, failure to repeal Section 3 would very easily impact the orderly development of other domestic energy and mineral resources that are essential to the country's economic and strategic futures. . . . The Section 3 repeal is not just a local issue or a regional issue or a geographic issue, not just a technical change. Rather Section 3 is of national concern.

A Sierra Club report on Section 3, entitled, *Old Leases - New Giveaways*, paints a different, but similarly dramatic, picture of a world without Section 3:

The repeal of Section 3 would allow these large (pre-FCLAA) leaseholders to continue indefinitely to speculate on vast quantities of public coal which Congress clearly intended to see either developed or given back by 1986. Although the repeal of Section 3 would clearly mean a substantial revenue loss to the taxpayers and a windfall to these large companies, no one knows how large this windfall would be.

To date, data are sparse to support the many arguments in favor of either repeal or enforcement of Section 3. Two reports contain most of the research and analysis that has been published on the Section 3 issue. One report was prepared by a consultant on behalf of the National Coal Association (NCA). Published in April, 1983 and entitled *An Evaluation of Selected Provisions of the Federal Coal Leasing Amendments Act of 1976*, it suggests that Section 3 should be repealed. The second report, *Old Leases - New Giveaways*, mentioned above and implying the opposite conclusion, was published in mid-1984 by the Sierra Club. Both reports rely heavily for data on two 1981 studies published by the U.S. Office of Technology Assessment, *An Assessment of Development and Production Potential of Federal Coal Leases* and *Patterns and Trends in Federal Coal Lease Ownership 1950 - 1980*.

Both the NCA and the Sierra Club reports argue that Section 3 will affect a large number of leases and lessees when the sanctions take hold beginning in 1986. That conclusion is central to the predictions of interest groups favoring repeal or enforcement. The Sierra Club report estimates that the majority of more than 200 non-producing leases, covering 7 of the 16 billion tons of coal under lease, are likely to face Section 3 sanctions in 1986. The NCA report places 385 leases covering more than 70 per cent of the acreage included in pre-FCLAA leases in an "inactive" category and potentially subject to Section 3 sanctions. More than 80 per cent of the companies holding pre-FCLAA leases had at least one lease in the inactive category.

KEY ARGUMENTS FOR AND AGAINST REPEAL

Several theories and arguments appear frequently in the testimonies, statements, and reports of interest groups favoring the repeal or the enforcement of Section 3. The most commonly cited arguments are outlined briefly below, each followed by its principal rebuttal argument.

ARGUMENTS IN FAVOR OF SECTION 3 REPEAL

SECTION 3 IS NO LONGER NEEDED
TO PREVENT SPECULATION

A major objective of Section 3 was to prevent lease speculation. The NCA report notes that leaseholdings by unincorporated individuals and land-holding companies, two lessee categories assumed to be populated by speculators, declined sharply from 17 per cent in 1970 to less than 4 per cent in 1982. The report concluded that " . . . the current ownership is almost exclusively by large companies with a current or eventual need for the coal resources for their own use or companies with a financial capability and technical know-how to produce coal for sale to large users."

Citing that change in ownership patterns, some people argue that lease speculation, perhaps once a problem, is no longer a concern. In this light, Section 3 becomes a solution without a problem. Furthermore, some people believe that Section 3 could actually have an opposite effect from its objective to prevent speculation. As the 1986 deadline approaches, companies capable of mining coal but unable to find markets might assign their leases to speculators without mining intentions rather than face the Section 3 sanctions.

On the other side are those who argue the speculation issue should be assessed by coal production statistics, not by ownership patterns. They assert that large companies operating coal mines elsewhere can still be guilty of speculation with public land leases. Indeed, some of the mining companies holding the largest number of leases are producing coal from only a few of them. To these people, the fact that about 80 per cent of all leases are still not in production suggests that lease speculation continues and sanctions against lessees not producing coal from the leases is warranted.

SECTION 3 WILL CAUSE A FLOOD OF COAL
ON THE MARKET

This suggests that companies will prematurely open coal mines to achieve commercial production and avoid the Section 3 sanction. Mined coal would flood an already glutted market forcing some competitors out of business and fostering inefficient production patterns and misallocation of the resource. The NCA report estimates an overcapacity of 53

15

million tons per year will exist in 1986 compared to market demand. If all pre-FCLAA lessees rushed to meet the Section 3 commercial production requirement as currently defined in Federal regulations, another 53 million tons of excess capacity would be created. The total overcapcity of 106 million tons would constitute more than one-third of projected coal demand of 315 million tons.

One counterargument is that few lessees would choose to open new mines as a method of avoiding Section 3 because prospects of profitably marketing coal would be dim. A more likely alternative, the argument goes, is they would relinquish or assign nonproducing leases. A corollary argument notes that many of the companies lobbying for a repeal because of a soft coal market also lobby for increased new coal leasing because of an alleged shortage of leased reserves. To many people, these two positions do not seem to be consistent with each other.

SECTION 3 WILL CAUSE COAL SHORTAGES

Some people project that enforcement of Section 3, rather than leading to a flood of unneeded coal on the market, will cause coal shortages. This argument assumes many lessees will opt to relinquish their leases. Thus, the number of competitors for new coal supply contracts will drop, and the number of active mines will diminish. For example, in testimony presented by the NCA and the American Mining Congress before the Senate Energy and Mineral Resources Subcommitee, the groups argued that the supply of Federal coal was barely sufficient to meet coal demand during the next ten years. If many leases are forfeited because of Section 3, they predict that " . . . fewer than two bidders per (coal supply) contract would be available for these same ten years of coal demand. In other words, Section 3 has the distinct possibility of effectively destroying competition in the sale of western coal."

The principal counterargument relies on supply-demand projections that predict a continuing overcapacity within the western coal industry. For example, a draft Environmental Statement published by the Department of Interior in February, 1985 predicts a coal production overcapacity until the year 2000 in every western coal supply region. If such predictions are correct, the relinquishment of Section 3 is unlikely to create coal shortages. Moreover, in the event shortages did appear, the counterargument notes that new leases can be issued to permit industry to expand in a timely fashion.

THE SECTION 3 SANCTION IS PUNITIVE

Many people argue that the prohibition against acquisition of any lease under the Mineral Leasing Act is an extreme and punitive action against pre-FCLAA leases that does not apply to other lessees of western mineral resources. Senator Frank Murkowski, for example, questions: "Why, for instance, should a company be prohibited from receiving a Federal oil and gas lease in Alaska if it has failed to produce commercial quantitites of coal from a Federal coal lease in Montana?" More pointedly, a Vice-President at Coastal States Energy complained in testimony: "The whole approach is one of punitiveness. In effect what they are saying is if you have the audacity to try and mine Federal coal, we are going to treat you like a second class citizen."

While it is true that lessees for other resources covered by the Mineral Leasing Act do not face the sanction contained in Section 3 for pre-FCLAA coal lessees, a counterargument notes that those non-coal lessees often face other harsh penalties for non-production. Noncompetitive oil and gas leases, for example, are simply cancelled if they are not in production or under active exploration within five years. Similiarly, post-FCLAA coal leases are terminated if they are not in production within ten years.

SECTION 3 WILL DIMINISH COMPETITITON FOR AND DEVELOPMENT OF OTHER RESOURCES

The basis for this argument is the assumption that many companies facing Section 3 sanctions also participate in leasing other resources under the Mineral Leasing Act. It further assumes that many of those companies would opt to retain their non-producing coal leases and thus lose the right to bid for leases for other resources.

If those assumptions are true, Section 3 could have a major effect on western resource development. Loss of potential bidders could diminish competition in western mineral industries, increase opportunities for speculators to acquire leases, and potentially slow the development of such vital resources as oil or natural gas. To support this scenario, the NCA report cites the following:

Section 3 leaseholders have been highly instrumental in maintaining competititon in federal mineral lease sales of all types. They were active bidders in at least 20 of the 35 onshore oil and gas lease sales analyzed, submitting a minimum of 48 bids; they were high bidders on 6 of the 8 other mineral resource sales held recently and are leaseholders for 72 per cent of federal leases of four of these resources and 21 per cent of the fifth.

The counterargument rests on the assumption that, given the choice, most lessees would opt to preserve the right to bid for other mineral resources rather than hold onto non-producing coal leases. With that in mind, testimony by the Western Organization of Resource Councils asserts that "Exxon is not going to get out of the oil and gas business. Mobil is not going to get out of the oil and gas business. If push comes to shove, these people will turn in their leases." Moreover, some people note the Section 3 sanction is not as broad as it appears. Offshore oil and gas leasing, for example, is not regulated by the Mineral Leasing Act. Also, lease acquisititon by assignment from another lessee are unlikely to be curtailed because of Section 3.

FEDERAL AND STATE REVENUES WILL BE REDUCED IF SECTION 3 IS ENFORCED

Federal and state governments share coal leasing income resulting from payments of bonuses by lessees to acquire leases, from annual rental payments, and from royalties paid per ton of coal mined. One basis for the argument to repeal Section 3 is that rental and royalty payments will be lost from leases relinquished because of Section 3.

The counterargument notes that FCLAA requires higher royalty and rental rates than are contained in most pre-FCLAA leases, and the law requires fair market value be obtained from bonus bids at lease sales. The argument posits that if pre-FCLAA leases are relinquished, new leases can be issued that would generate a higher revenue flow to federal and state governments from bonuses as well as royalties and rentals.

THE 10-YEAR DEADLINE IN SECTION 3 IS TOO SHORT

Some people suggest the ten year "clock" contained in Section 3 does not offer pre-FCLAA lessees sufficient time to bring coal leases into production. A report prepared to supplement testimony by Peabody Coal Co., for example, estimates an average of 12 years is needed after a lease is issued to bring a mine into full production. Other testimony notes that laws enacted after FCLAA and unknown to Congress when it set the ten year deadline in Section 3, especially the Surface Mining Control and Reclamation Act of 1977, have created new regulatory requirements that frequently add years to mine development. While those arguments do not suggest Section 3 necessarily be repealed, they do support the notion that Section 3 as it now stands is punitive.

Critics of the short deadline argument cite other studies and examples that suggest ten years is sufficient time for an earnest developer to bring a mine into production. The 1981 OTA assessment, for example, estimates that 7 to 12 years are needed for mine development. Another counterargument is that pre-FCLAA lessees generally have held their leases for many years prior to FCLAA during which they should have been working on mine development plans. Moreover, current regulations require only production of commercial quantities of coal, not full production capability within ten years to avoid Section 3 sanctions.

ARGUMENTS FOR ENFORCEMENT OF SECTION 3

Most of the counterarguments cited above against the various rationales used to support repeal of Section 3, of course, can stand alone as arguments in favor of enforcement of Section 3. Thus, the pro-enforcement arguments discussed so far are that Section 3 is still needed to fight speculation; that it will not disrupt western coal markets by either increasing production or lowering competition; that it will not hinder development of other mineral resources; that it is fair, not punitive; that it will increase, rather than lower revenue to state and federal governments; and that its ten year deadline is reasonable. In addition, several other arguments, discussed below, are frequently cited in support of Section 3.

SECTION 3 CORRECTS A BIAS AGAINST POST-FCLAA LESSEES

Most pre-FCLAA leases were cheaply acquired and contain lower royalty and rental requirements than post-FCLAA leases. Furthermore, they do not contain the ten year diligent development requirement of post-FCLAA leases. They do contain a diligent development clause, but that clause does not include a deadline for production. One argument in favor of Section 3 asserts that the sanctions help to equalize the position of pre- and post-FCLAA lessees and, thus, foster competition within the western coal industry. According to testimony of the National Wildlife

Federation, through its repeal effort, pre-FCLAA lessees are attempting " . . . to bootstrap onto the extended diligence requirements and are asking Congress to help them."

Moreover, some people observe that since 1976, Section 3 has presumably influenced the action of bidders at post-FCLAA lease sales and affected business transactions involving leases. A change in Section 3 could unfairly reward lessees who speculated that Section 3 would be repealed.

Others counter that post-FCLAA lessees knew about their ten-year diligence deadlines while pre-FCLAA lessees had the ten year Section 3 deadline and sanctions thrust unfairly upon them. They argue further that the fact that Congress changed the leasing laws in 1976 does not mean that pre-FCLAA lessees should lose whatever advantages they may have by virtue of their early participation in the program.

REPEAL OF SECTION 3 WOULD OFFER WINDFALL PROFITS TO PRE-FCLAA LESSEES

Windfall profits to the large companies — especially the major oil companies — is a major theme of the Sierra Club report denouncing efforts to repeal Section 3. The argument is based on the fact that most pre-FCLAA leases were obtained very cheaply, while bidders for post-FCLAA leases are required by law to pay fair market value. Also pre-FCLAA leases contain low royalty requirements, often 20 cents per ton, while post-FCLAA leases usually require royalty payments of more than $1.00 per ton. The Sierra Club reports estimates that seven major oil companies control 45 per cent of the coal reserves included in leases that are not likely to be in production by 1986. Such companies, the report avers, stand to profit excessively if they are allowed to hold onto the leases after 1986 because their mining costs — which include lease acquisition costs and royalties — will be less than the costs facing the post-FCLAA competitors.

The counterargument accepts that pre-FCLAA leases were often cheaply acquired, but notes that royalty and rental rates of pre-FCLAA leases can be raised to match those of post-FCLAA leases when their lease terms are subject to adjustment, although some companies are challenging the Department of Interior's readjustment powers and policies. Thus, the advantage will be erased over time. By one estimate, 80 per cent of the pre-FCLAA leases will have undergone readjustment by 1987.

SECTION 3 WILL HELP PREVENT ENVIRONMENTAL DAMAGE

Pre-FCLAA leases generally were issued prior to the era when the government performed comprehensive land use planning procedures to ensure multiple resource use on public lands and minimize environmental conflicts from resource uses. As a result, leases were issued without regard to environmental problems that might occur during and after coal mining. At the time when Section 3 was first being debated in Congress, environmental concern over coal development in some western regions was so high some people asserted that mining would be akin to declaring those regions "national sacrifice areas" because of the environmental damage mining would entail.

These facts support another argument in favor of Section 3. This argument suggests that Section 3 provides a means by which to force relinquishment of leases issued in environmentally-sensitive areas into the public domain. Then future land use planning programs can ensure the environmental values are protected.

On the other side are those who argue that lessees mining coal must comply with many environmental protection laws including the National Environmental Policy Act and the Surface Mining Control and Reclamation Act. Even though the leases were issued without regard to environmental issues, they argue that existing laws are sufficiently strict to protect the environment during mining.

SECTION 3 WILL PERMIT A HEALTHY "HOUSE-CLEANING" OF LEASES

The Department of Interior issued leases essentially on a first-come, first-served basis to companies and individuals requesting them from 1920 to 1970. The boundaries of lease tracts were surveyed, but few attempts were made by the DOI to ascertain the quantity or quality of coal contained in the lease tracts. Moreover, many early leases were for small isolated tracts of land containing coal recoverable only by underground mining. Those leases sustained mines serving local markets that, in many cases, no longer exist and use mining technology that is no longer cost-effective. Thus, it seems logical that national energy planners would know much less about the coal contained in pre-FCLAA lease tracts and the ability of those tracts to supply western coal demand than they know about post-FCLAA lease tracts that have been extensively studied prior to leasing.

Some people argue that lack of knowledge about pre-FCLAA leases not only encumbers land use planning but also hampers accurate coal supply forecasting and the projection of the need for new leasing. Moreover, uncertainty about potential adverse effects of development of pre-FCLAA leases could lead to a tightening of land use requirements for all lessees in order to lessen possible cumulative impacts from mining. These people argue that Section 3 will help clear out the back-log of pre-FCLAA leases, after which, as the Sierra Club report notes, " . . . the Government could replan and reoffer the coal reserves in competitive sales and at current royalty rates. In these cases, the enforcement of Section 3 may actually contribute to the development prospects for some Federal coal reserves."

The counterargument essentially denies a house-cleaning problem exists. It asserts that nearly as much is known about the development prospects of pre-FCLAA lease tracts as post-FCLAA tracts or unleased coal-bearing lands. Thus, the back-log of pre-FCLAA leases does not hinder DOI planning efforts or energy forecasts.

REPEAL OF SECTION 3 WILL UNDERMINE THE ALREADY ERODING DILIGENCE PROGRAM

Section 3 is one of several provisions in FCLAA designed to ensure that leased land is brought into production in a timely fashion. The diligence provision also sets a ten-year deadline for commercial production. Since 1976, however, regulations defining diligence and commercial quantities have been weakened. For example, regulations promulgated in May, 1976 required all existing lease tracts to produce 2.5 per cent of its recoverable coal reserves by June 1, 1986. That regulation was changed in two ways in 1982. Pre-FCLAA lessees are now required to produce just one per cent of leased reserves and the deadline for production has been extended until ten years after the date of the first readjustment of lease terms after passage of FCLAA. Commercial production for post-FCLAA leases has also been reduced from 2.5 per cent to 1.0 per cent by the Reagan administration. Some people argue that repeal of Section 3 would further erode the diligent development program, permit the reintroduction of land speculation, and undermine public confidence in the leasing program.

The counterargument is a statement of economic theory asserting that diligence programs themselves have no place in the leasing program. It assumes the most efficient development of coal will occur when the fewest restrictions are placed on the actions of developers. The argument concludes that diligence programs and Section 3 will promote inefficient allocation of coal resources because they interfere with a free market.

A NEW ANALYSIS OF THE IMPACTS OF SECTION 3

The methodology used in this study includes the examination of lease ownership changes, not analyzed in other studies published to date or discussed in Congressional testimony, that affect whether or not a lessee will face Section 3 sanctions beginning in 1986. Changes in lease and lessee ownership will, or may, reset the Section 3 ten-year clock and release certain leaseholders from Section 3 sanctions in 1986. Other studies and Section 3 analysts acknowledge that lease ownership changes, as well as mine development status, affect suspectibility of lessees to Section 3. The research, however, has been limited to projections of Section 3 effects based on mine development projections alone. This report, therefore, presents original research that is more likely to reflect the true stakes.

Data about lease ownership changes were obtained directly from primary sources; specifically, lease case files and serial register books housed at western state offices of the Bureau of Land Management (BLM) within the Department of Interior. Lessee ownership changes were identified during a review of business and finance publications such as Moody's Industrial Guide. A complete discussion of the methodology appears in Appendix A.

The principal objectives of this analysis were to identify all pre-FCLAA leases within a seven state study region, assess the likelihood that the current lessee of each lease will face the sanctions provided by Section 3, and to examine the implications of that assessment with regard to the arguments in favor of repeal or enforcement of Section 3. The seven states are North Dakota, Montana, Wyoming, Utah, Colorado, New Mexico, and Oklahoma. Over 95 per cent of all federal coal lease tracts are located in those states.

A lease catalogue published in 1981 by the Office of Technology Assessment allowed the identification of 516 pre-FCLAA leases covering 761,668 acres to be identified. The review of BLM files indicated, however, that 16 of the leases have been voluntarily relinquished since 1976, thereby reducing leased acreage to 761,668 acres and the number of pre-FCLAA leases to 500. As the relinquishments have reduced the number of pre-FCLAA leases potentially subject to Section 3, new leasing since enactment of FCLAA has expanded the number of leases not subject to Section 3 in 1986. Seventeen per cent of the leases existing as of the end of 1984 represent post-FCLAA leases not subject to Section 3 in 1986.

All further analysis in this study addresses only the 500 currently existing pre-FCLAA leases. Once identified, the second step is to assess the susceptibility of the lessee of each lease to Section 3 based on mine development and ownership criteria established by the statute. Three categories were established as follows:

- *Low chance* of sanctions. This group includes leases whose owners are unlikely to face Section 3 sanctions beginning in 1986 because the lease tracts are currently in production or part of mining plans that have been approved by the U.S. Office of Surface Mining (OSM) *or* because the leases have been assigned since 1976 to another lessee unaffiliated with the lessee at the time FCLAA was enacted.

- *Uncertain chance* of sanctions. This category includes leases that mine plans have been submitted to, but as of mid-1981 not approved by, the Office of Surface Mining, or leases that have been affected by an ownership change involving less than a complete 100 per cent assignment to a party unaffiliated with the lessee in 1976. The susceptibility of the current lessee to Section 3 in 1986 is unclear on both development and ownership grounds.
- *High chance* of sanctions. This group includes currently undeveloped leases that are not included in mine plans approved or pending before OSM and that have not undergone any significant changes in ownership since 1976. At the beginning of 1985, the owners of these lessees appear likely to face Section 3 sanctions beginning in 1986.

The conclusions of the asssessment and analysis undertaken in this study follow.

THE SCOPE OF SECTION 3 HAS BEEN GREATLY OVERESTIMATED

The assessment process identified just 117 leases covering 140,998 acres — or a mere 19 per cent of the land included in pre-FCLAA leases — as leases whose owners face a *high chance* of being subject to Section 3 sanctions in 1986. The results of the classification appear in Table 1. Furthermore, less than one-third of the current owners of federal coal leases — 45 out of a total of about 160 lessees — hold one or more leases in the high chance category.

Another 25 per cent of the acres covered by pre-FCLAA leases involve 108 leases that fall into the *uncertain chance* category with regard to the susceptibility of the current lessee to Section 3 sanctions in 1986. The owners of a majority of pre-FCLAA leases, 275 — covering 428,119 acres, or 56 per cent of of the land included in pre-FCLAA leases — are categorized in the *low chance* group and are likely to be exempt from Section 3 in 1986.

Table I
Susceptibility of Lessees
of PRE-FCLAA Leases to Section 3

	# LEASES	# ACRES	% OF TOTAL ACRES
HIGH CHANCE	117	140,998	19%
UNCERTAIN CHANCE	108	192,551	25%
LOW CHANCE	275	428,119	56%
Total	500	761,668	100%

The identification of such a small number of leases as highly likely to meet the criteria triggering Section 3 sanctions in 1986 stands in sharp contrast to the findings of both the National Coal Association and the Sierra Club studies. It also differs from the statements made by many organizations and individuals standing on both sides of the controversy. Even if the lessees of all the leases falling in the uncertain chance category do, in fact, face Section 3 in 1986, ownership of less than half of all pre-FCLAA leases, or 44 per cent, would trigger Section 3 sanctions. This is compared to estimates of 70 per cent cited in other studies. As explained below, the actual number of leases triggering Section 3 sanctions in 1986 could be well below 44 per cent, but it is likely to be greater than 20 per cent. This study also finds that the minority of lessees, somewhere between 25 per cent and 40 per cent, are likely to face Section 3 sanctions in 1986, compared with estimates in other studies as high as 80 per cent.

The reason for divergence of results of other studies published to date lies in the lack of investigation into the effects of ownership changes. The ownership analysis in this study found that 64 per cent of all pre-FCLAA leases have experienced some significant change in ownership since 1976. For many leases, several ownership changes have occurred since 1976; in total, this analysis identified 497 ownership changes, including changes affecting more than one lease, out of a total of 500 leases, or an average of nearly one ownership change per lease.

Examination of the relative importance of ownership changes to development status for leases in the low chance category reveals that ownership change is almost as important as development status as a determinant of susceptibility of pre-FCLAA leases to Section 3 in 1986. As shown in Table 2, development status — inclusion in approved plans — was determined to exempt the owners of 160 leases from Section 3. Ownership changes — lease assignments among unaffiliated lessees — were found to exempt 147 leases. (Some leases were exempted by both criteria). Other studies, limited to examination of development status, failed to identify the 115 leases whose owners were found in this study to be exempt from Section 3 effects in 1986 solely on the basis of ownership change criteria.

Some pre-FCLAA leases had been assigned more than once since 1976; in total, 177 assignments among unaffiliated companies were identified involving the 147 leases (see Table 2). Some transactions involved the same two assignor and assignee companies simultaneously transfering ownership of more than one lease; 79 distinct assignment transactions involving one or more leases account for the 177 lease assignments.

Table II
Effect of Lease Assignments
on Susceptibility to Section 3

NUMBER OF LEASES EXEMPT FROM SECTION 3 IN 1986 BECAUSE OF POST-FCLAA LEASE ASSIGNMENTS	147
TOTAL NUMBER OF LEASE ASSIGNMENTS	177
NUMBER OF UNIQUE ASSIGNMENT TRANSACTIONS	79
NUMBER OF LEASES EXEMPT FROM SECTION 3 BECAUSE OF DEVELOPMENT STATUS	160

Examination of lease records revealed that approximately 15 leases are in the process of being assigned, with the assignments awaiting BLM approval to become effective. These assignments, plus new assignments filed and approved between January 1, 1985 and the Section 3 deadline of August 4, 1986, are likely to further increase the number of lessees exempt from Section 3 in 1986 on ownership grounds. If the pace of assignment activity from 1976 through 1984 continues until August 4, 1986, another 28 leases will be assigned before the Section 3 deadline. More likely, the pace will accelerate.

THE FATE OF THE UNCERTAIN CATEGORY LEASES IS A CRITICAL FACTOR DETERMINING THE IMPACTS OF SECTION 3

Over 100 leases, covering 25 per cent of all pre-FCLAA lease acreage, were assigned in this study to the uncertain chance category for one of two reasons. The first was uncertain prospects for development by virtue of their inclusion in a mine plan pending approval in mid-1981 by OSM. The existence of a mine plan suggests that a bona fide development project is anticipated by the lessee. But the lack of OSM approval of the plan suggests that production of commercial quantities might not be achieved by 1986. A total of 17 out of 108 leases were placed in the uncertain category on the basis of development criteria.

Most of the uncertain category leases drew their designation on the basis of unclear implications of ownership changes that affect them. This study uncovered five distinct types of ownership changes, affecting 102 leases, that might or might not have a bearing on the susceptibility of the current lessees to Section 3 sanctions. A total of 169 uncertain ownership changes involve those 102 leases, reflecting 28 unique ownership transactions. These ownership changes alter who has ultimate control of leases, but reflect something less than a 100 per cent assignment of leases among unaffiliated companies. The susceptibility to Section 3 depends on the legal interpretation of the relationship between the ownership change and the "holds and has held" statutory language of Section 3.

• *Acquisition of leaseholding company.* The acquisition of a company that holds federal coal leases by another company results in a change in the ultimate corporate decision-maker without necessarily changing the lessee itself. This study identified 15 corporate acquisitions of leaseholding companies between 1976 and the end of 1984. Nine out of the 15 mergers involve major oil or natural gas companies. For example, Kemmerer Coal Co., a lessee, was acquired by Gulf Oil Corp., a lessee on its own, which in turn was acquired by the Chevron Corp.; Plateau Mining Co. was acquired by Getty Oil Corp. which in turn was acquired by Texaco Oil Corp.; and Belco Petroleum Corp. was acquired by Internorth Corp. Other acquisitions, such as the sale of Utah International, Inc. by its former parent, General Electric Corp., to Broken Hill Proprietary, Ltd., do not involve oil companies, but do affect companies holding significant quantities of leased coal reserves.

• *Acquisition followed by corporate reorganization.* In some cases, the merging of two companies following a corporate acquisition involves an internal reorganization that results in the renaming of what once was a leaseholding company into a new corporate entity. When this occurs, a new name appears on the record of lease ownership, but the transaction is not the same as a 100 per cent transfer of lease ownership through assignment. For example, Getty Oil Corp. acquired Energy Fuels Co., then Colorado's biggest independent coal producer, in 1981. The new subsidiary was renamed the Colorado Yampa Coal Co. and, after a corporate reshuffling, the leases were assigned to Getty Minerals Co.

- *Acquisition or assignment affecting partial lease interests.* The ownership of about 75 federal coal leases is shared among two or more companies. Each of these companies holds an undivided interest in a percentage of the lease. This study identified a number of instances since 1976 where lessees have assigned partial interest in leases or have been acquired by other companies, while the other owner or owners have retained their interests. For example, in December 1984, Jane Aul assigned a 33 per cent interest in a Colorado lease to Powderhorn Properties. The remaining 67 per cent interest is retained by Pitkin Iron Corp. In another case, Gulf Oil Corp.'s acquisition of Kemmerer Coal in 1981 affected ten Utah leases jointly owned by Kemmerer and Consolidation Coal Co., a subsidiary of CONOCO, Inc. Within a year, the ownership pattern was jolted again as DuPont acquired Consolidation Coal's parent company.

- *Assignments involving changes in joint venture partnerships or other multi-corporate business arrangements.* This study found a few changes in the structure of lease ownership as a result of the reshuffling of partners in joint ventures or as a result of lease ownership restructuring involving the same controlling parent companies. For example, in 1982 Western Coal Co., a joint venture of Public Service Company of New Mexico and Tucson Electric Company, was dissolved. Four New Mexico leases held by Western Coal were subsequently assigned to two companies, each with an undivided 50 per cent interest. The two companies, Paragon Resources Co. and Valencia Energy Co., are subsidiaries respectively of Public Service Co. of New Mexico and Tucson Electric Co. Thus, a lease assignment has occurred and a joint venture ownership structure has been replaced by an undivided multi-corporate ownership structure. But the controlling companies remained unchanged.

- *Segregation of a lease into two leases under control of the same company.* A coal lessee, with the approval of the DOI, is permitted to divide the acreage contained in a lease into two subunits. A new lease can be created for one of the subunits and assigned to a company while the lessee retains control of the other subunit. When the new lease was assigned to an unaffiliated company, this study assumed the Section 3 clock would begin at the date of assignment for the lessee of the segregated lease. Such leases were assigned to the low chance category. When the segregated lease was assigned to a subsidiary or an affiliate of the company controlling the original lease, however, this study designated the new lease to the uncertain chance category.

Legal interpretations given to these five types of ownership changes will determine the susceptibility of the lessees to Section 3 sanctions in

1986. The determination will have a major impact on the ultimate effect of Section 3. Several of the largest leaseholding companies in terms of leased acreage, for example Utah International, Inc., Peabody Coal Co., Consolidation Coal Co., and Gulf Oil Corp., have a significant portion of leases affected by one or more of the ownership changes. The effect this will have on Section 3 is unclear. The future role of companies in the mineral leasing program depends, in part, on the definition placed on the ownership changes the leases have undergone.

If all of the ownership changes in the uncertain category are assumed to have no bearing on Section 3, most of the lessees will face a high chance of being subject to Section 3 sanctions in 1986. The potential for negative and positive consequences, such as disruption in western coal markets and lease speculation, will then be increased. On the other hand, the opposite interpretation would result in a reassignment of the uncertain leases to the low chance category and lessen the potential effects of Section 3 enforcement, both positive and negative. Furthermore, that interpretation could expose loopholes to other pre-FCLAA lessees that now hold lessees in the high chance category. The lessees could then use the loopholes to escape Section 3 sanctions without losing control over the leases.

Despite the critical need to resolve questions about the relationship between the various types of ownership changes and the statutory language of Section 3, no study or Congressional testimony to date has addressed the issue. Yet, until that debate takes place, neither side on the Section 3 issue can claim to understand the true stakes presented by that provision of law.

THE PUNITIVE ASPECTS OF SECTION 3 HAVE BEEN OVERPLAYED; SECTION 3 HELPS TO CORRECT A BIAS AGAINST POST-FCLAA LESSEES

Two opposing arguments are that Section 3 is an unfair and punitive action thrust upon pre-FCLAA lessees, and it will help eliminate the unfair advantages that pre-FCLAA lessees enjoy. The evidence collected in this study sheds some light on the relative merits of each argument and finds more support for the second than the first.

Studies to date, because they have not examined the ownership issue, have understated the options available to pre-FCLAA lessees to protect their interests while complying with Section 3. Lease assignments involving pre-FCLAA leases have in fact been common since 1976. And, with each assignment, the Section 3 clock restarts. The similar restarting of the clock might result from some or all of the other types of ownership changes in the uncertain category.

While ownership changes do not exempt lessees from Section 3 permanently, the restarting of the clock is important for several reasons. First, the existing option for pre-FCLAA lessees to avoid the production requirement of Section 3 by virtue of ownership changes makes the provision less punitive than its critics, who make no mention of that option, suggest. Secondly, each new owner of pre-FCLAA lease obtained since 1976 through lease assignment or some other mechanism of ownership change, acquired that lease in full knowledge that a Section 3 clock would begin upon lease acquisition. Pre-FCLAA lessees might have had Section 3 thrust upon them, but the new owners can claim no such unfair treatment. Thirdly, the restarting of the Section 3 clock with every ownership change puts those new lessees on a more equal footing with companies that acquired new leases since passage of FCLAA. New owners of the pre-FCLAA leases in many cases still have the advantage of lower royalty and rental provisions in their leases. But the clicking of the Section 3 clock is somewhat comparable to the ten year deadline for diligent production contained in all post-FCLAA leases.

SPECULATION IS NOT DEAD, AND SECTION 3 MIGHT NOT KILL IT

This study identified approximately 30 pre-FCLAA coal leases now owned by unincorporated individuals bereft of the financial or technical ability to mine coal. This is a significant reduction in leaseholdings by individuals, most of whom are assumed to be speculators. In 1970 they controlled 83 leases. The current holdings of six per cent of all pre-FCLAA leases, however, are not yet insignificant. It is unclear what effect the Section 3 deadline may have had on the decision of former leaseholding speculators to assign the leases to bona fide developers. But whatever effect there may have been would be lost with the repeal of Section 3. Many companies holding leases in the high chance category have controlled them for so long without producing coal that they too could be accused of speculating. These considerations undercut the arguments that speculation is no longer a problem of concern to the leasing program.

Furthermore, an analysis of current ownership patterns suggests that Section 3 could have an important influence on the future of the leases now held by individuals. As shown in Table 3, 93 per cent of the leased land controlled by individuals falls into the high chance category. This is the highest concentration of leaseholdings of any of the 11 business categories examined. Therefore, individual speculators, as a group, feel the pressure of Section 3 more than any other business. This further supports the logic of Section 3 as a tool to prevent speculation.

On the other hand, unless speculators holding leases in the high chance category hope to acquire new mineral leases in the West, the Section 3 sanctions they will face are toothless. The fact that most individuals control only one lease and many individuals acquired the leases decades ago suggests they are currently not very active in western mineral lease acquisition and would be unaffected by Section 3. Furthermore, if the lease assignment price drops low enough as some pre-FCLAA leases elect to assign their leases rather than face Section 3 sanctions, there is nothing to discourage new speculators, as Section 3 currently stands, from acquiring them.

Table 3
Susceptibility of Federal Leases to Section 3 by Business Activity of Lessee

BUSINESS CATEGORY	EXEMPT LEASES		UNCERTAIN LEASES		SECTION 3 LEASES		TOTAL ACRES
	Acres	%	Acres	%	Acres	%	
Utilities	82372	54%	10232	7%	60688	40%	153292
Oil majors	93549	66%	37599	27%	9958	7%	141106
Nonres. Divers. Co's.	19465	30%	44153	69%	561	1%	64179
Steel Co's.	15568	28%	0	0%	39446	72%	55014
Peabody Holding Co.	4307	10%	40465	90%	0	0%	44772
Oil & Gas Co's.	23754	60%	9929	25%	6036	15%	39719
Metals & Mining Co's.	18490	47%	20616	53%	0	0%	39106
Natural Gas Co's.	23480	81%	4718	16%	955	3%	29153
Coal Co's.	20151	72%	280	1%	7409	27%	27840
Individuals	360	6%	80	1%	6073	93%	6513
Other Co's.	126623	79%	24479	15%	9872	6%	160974
TOTAL	428119	56%	192551	25%	140998	19%	761668

REPEAL OF SECTION 3 WILL NOT BE A WINDFALL TO THE BIG OIL COMPANIES

This study could find little support for the argument that repeal of Section 3 will offer a financial windfall to the major oil and gas companies. Referring to Table 3, it can be seen that only one per cent of the lease acreage held by major oil companies falls in the high chance category, even though those companies control 18 per cent of all pre-FCLAA lease acreage. Similarly major natural gas companies have only three per cent of their lease acreage in the high chance category and only 15 per cent of the leased acreage held by smaller oil and gas companies is in that category. The leaseholdings of all three industry groups falling in the high chance category are well below the average of 18 per cent.

This finding, coupled with the broader finding that fewer lessees are likely to face Section 3 sanctions in 1986 compared to the numbers predicted, suggests that the postulated financial windfall to pre-FCLAA leases as a result of repeal of Section 3 may have been overstated to date. And the oil and gas industry may not be the major beneficiaries of such a windfall.

It is important to note, however, that the resolution of the status of the leases in the uncertain chance category will affect the impact of Section 3 on the major oil and gas companies. As shown in Table 3, 27 per cent of the acreage controlled by the major oil companies and 16 per cent of the acreage owned by natural gas companies falls in the uncertain chance category. If all this acreage ultimately is subject to Section 3, the effect of its enforcement on those industries would be increased. But the stake of oil and gas companies as far as their susceptibility to Section 3 would still be less than average among the 11 industry groups studied.

ENFORCEMENT OF SECTION 3 WILL NOT HINDER THE LEASING AND DEVELOPMENT OF OTHER MINERAL RESOURCES

Electric utilities and steel companies were found in this study to have the largest number of leases in the high chance category. Together they control 71 per cent of the acreage assigned to that category. Individually, 72 per cent of the acreage controlled by steel companies and 40 per cent of the acreage controlled by utilities falls into the high chance category. By comparison, as mentioned above, major oil and natural gas companies together have only 4 per cent of their acreage assigned to the high chance category.

Of the 11 industry groups analyzed, utilities and steel companies are among the least likely to be active bidders for non-coal leases under provisions of the Mineral Leasing Act. Therefore, the Section 3 sanction prohibiting violating companies from obtaining new leases under the Mineral Leasing Act is unlikely to have a major impact on lessees standing the highest probability of facing that sanction. Thus, arguments that Section 3 will undercut competitition for western mineral resources and hamper development of such important resources as oil and gas do not appear to be well founded.

If leases in the uncertain category are added to the high chance category, the nonresource-diversified and metal and mining industries and Peabody Coal Co. would also have a higher than average percentage of leases potentially susceptible to Section 3 sanctions beginning in 1986.

ENFORCEMENT OF SECTION 3 WILL NOT DISRUPT THE MAJOR WESTERN COAL SUPPLY MARKETS

Based on information obtained largely from the *Federal Coal Management Report* published by the Department of Interior for fiscal year 1983, this study estimates that over 80 per cent of the coal produced from public land in the West came from three regions; the Powder River Basin of Montana and Wyoming, the Green River region of Colorado, and the Uinta region of Utah.

Table 4 presents the results of an analysis of susceptibility of leases to Section 3 organized by geographical distribution among western coal regions. The table shows the following concentrations of high chance leased acreage in the major coal production regions mentioned above:

COAL REGION	% OF ACREAGE IN THE HIGH CHANCE CATEGORY
Powder River - Montana	4%
Powder River - Wyoming	11%
Green River - Colorado	5%
Uinta - Utah	13%
Average for all regions	19%

Each of the regions has a lower than average concentration of leases in the high chance category. This indicates that the number of leases in these regions whose owners are likely to face Section 3 is small. If the uncertain chance leases are grouped with high chance leases, each region, with the exception of the Wyoming portion of the Powder River Basin, would still have a lower percentage of leases than average. Therefore, enforcement of Section 3 is likely to have little impact in the major western coal production regions. However, it could have a greater impact elsewhere and possibly entail local adverse effects on the coal industry in other regions.

MANY HIGH CHANCE SECTION 3 LEASES ARE LOCATED IN ENVIRONMENTALLY-SENSITIVE AREAS

A corollary finding to the lack of concentration of high chance Section 3 leases in the major coal supply regions is that many high chance Section 3 leases are located in areas where little or no coal mining is currently taking place. This includes some environmentally-sensitive regions where strong opposition to coal mining on environmental grounds has been voiced.

Table 4
Susceptibility of Leases in Coal Production Regions to Section 3

STATE	PRODUCTION REGION	EXEMPT LEASES		UNCERTAIN LEASES		SECTION 3 LEASES		TOTAL ACRES
		Acres	%	Acres	%	Acres	%	
Colorado	Green River	29204	60%	17352	35%	2495	5%	49051
	Den-Raton — Colorado	962	96%	0	0%	40	4%	1002
	Uinta — Colorado	44572	63%	21801	31%	4483	6%	70856
Montana	Fort Union — Montana	0	0%	0	0%	6056	100%	6056
	Bull Mountain	0	0%	0	0%	160	100%	160
	Powder River — Montana	28937	96%	0	0%	1065	4%	30002
New Mexico	San Juan Basin	26898	66%	11791	29%	2150	5%	40839
	Den-Raton — New Mexico	161	80%	0	0%	40	20%	201
North Dakota	Fort Union — N. Dakota	12091	74%	40	0%	4232	26%	16363
Oklahoma	Western Interior	31260	43%	6862	10%	33939	47%	72061
Utah	Uinta — Utah	80050	70%	19528	17%	14915	13%	114493
	Southwest	34178	23%	64375	43%	52512	35%	151065
Wyoming	Yellowstone	0	0%	80	100%	0	0%	80
	Powder River — Wyoming	70880	55%	44057	34%	13880	11%	128817
	Hanna Basin	21773	97%	0	0%	640	3%	22413
	Rock Springs	39663	85%	2480	5%	4271	9%	46414
	Kemmerer-Big Horn	7490	64%	4185	35%	120	1%	11795
	TOTAL	428119	56%	192551	25%	140998	19%	761668

Southwest Utah is the clearest example to support this finding. This region contains by far the most acreage assigned to the high chance category, 37 per cent of the total acreage in that category. Coal development in Southwest Utah has been forcefully and successfully opposed, for more than a decade, by interest groups concerned about potential adverse impacts of development in this arid and remote region. It contains the highest concentration of national parks, national monuments, and wilderness areas anywhere in the United States, excluding Alaska. Many interest groups fear that mining this region will transform it into an industrial park, the equivalent of a "national sacrifice area" as far as its environmental values. Public opposition, to date, has defeated several industry proposals for coal mines and power plants in the region.

This suggests that enforcement of Section 3 might prevent development of coal resources in some areas of high environmental concern. It cannot address, however, the questions of whether or not the leases in such areas could be developed in compliance with existing environmental protection laws. Nor does it address the enforcement of Section 3 as an appriopriate mechanism to hamper development there.

THE TOTAL REVENUE TO FEDERAL AND WESTERN STATE TREASURIES FROM LEASING IS LIKELY TO BE HIGHER IF SECTION 3 IS ENFORCED THAN IF IT IS REPEALED

Under FCLAA, income from bonus bids, royalties, and rentals are divided equally between the federal government and the states in which leases are located. If Section 3 is enforced and all high chance leases are relinquished as a result of enforcement, federal and state governments will lose just the rentals lessees are required to pay on nonproducing leased acreage. Bonus bids have already been paid and royalty payments are not required because the relinquished leases, by definition, were nonproducing. Rental rates for pre-FCLAA leases are usually between $1 and $3 per acre per year. Assuming an average rental payment of $2 per acre per year, the relinquishment of all high chance leases would reduce rental payments by $282,000 per year. The distribution of revenue loss per state can be derived from the state-by-state breakdown of leased acreage contained in Table 5, by assigning $1 in annual revenue loss to each acre designated to the high chance category.

Western states would lose only 18 per cent of the total rental payments they receive from pre-FCLAA leases if all high chance leases are relinquished. The biggest bite into revenue would occur in Oklahoma, where 47 per cent of the leases are in the high chance category. The smallest impact would be felt in New Mexico. If all leases in the uncertain category are also relinquished, state rental revenue would decline by 44 per cent.

Impact on rental income itself would be small and impact on total revenue from leasing would be insignificant since rental payments are by far the least lucrative source of revenue derived from leasing. In fiscal year 1983, for example, total rental payments from all leases — including

Table 5

Location of Leases by State According to Susceptibility to Section 3

STATE	EXEMPT LEASES		UNCERTAIN LEASES		SECTION 3 LEASES		TOTAL ACRES
	Acres	%	Acres	%	Acres	%	
Colorado	74898	62%	39153	32%	7018	6%	121069
Montana	28937	80%	80	0%	7281	20%	36298
New Mexico	26899	66%	11791	29%	2190	5%	40880
North Dakota	12091	74%	40	0%	4232	26%	16363
Utah	114228	43%	83903	32%	67427	25%	265558
Wyoming	139806	67%	50722	24%	18911	9%	209439
Oklahoma	31260	43%	6862	10%	33939	47%	72061
TOTAL	428119	56%	192551	25%	140998	19%	761668

post-FCLAA leases — was in the neighborhood of $1.0 million to $1.5 million dollars. By contrast, bonus bids paid for new coal leases issued during the year totalled $26.2 million, and royalty payments based on coal mined during the year totalled $56.7 million.

Thus, enforcement of Section 3 in the short-term is likely to reduce revenues from leasing by less 2 per cent. In the long-term, the revenue flow would be likely to increase because the relinquished leases could be re-offered at new competitive lease sales. And, as the data above indicate, bonus bids are many times larger than the rental payments likely to be received.

THE 10-YEAR DEADLINE UNDER SECTION 3 GENERALLY IS NOT UNREASONABLE

Many industry officials have complained that the ten-year deadline for production contained in Section 3 is unreasonably short. Development of coal mines, they say, can often require 12 or even 15 years to complete. Evidence in this study suggests that the ten year timeframe in Section 3 is not unfair. Most pre-FCLAA leases have been held by their current owner for many years prior to 1976 during which they were required to act to develop them even though there was no established deadline for development.

Calculations performed in this study reveal that the average date of issuance of leases assigned to the high chance category was July 26, 1960, or a little more than 26 years before the Section 3 deadline. More importantly, perhaps, the average date of acquisition of leases in the high chance category by their current owners — the ones that might face the Section 3 sanctions — was December 20, 1966. In other words, in 1986, when the Section 3 sanctions will begin to be applied, the lessees facing those sanctions will have owned, and presumably will have been diligently working to develop, their leases for an average of nearly 20 years. This is many years longer than even the most conservative mine development timeframe offered during the Section 3 debate.

SECTION 3 ENFORCEMENT COULD ASSIST IN PRE-FCLAA LEASE HOUSECLEANING

A nonrigorous review of the location, size, and ownership histories of pre-FCLAA leases conducted during the course of this study suggests that many leases contained in the high chance category are no longer economically viable mining prospects. They are small and isolated tracts that no longer can serve coal markets, or have been embroiled in lengthy legal controversies. For example, a lessee in Montana has been cited for misuse of the tract as a hunting lodge rather than a mining property. A lease in New Mexico was the center of a battle over ownership that at one time or another involved about 10 different parties all claiming to be the legitimate lessee. Several leases in the high chance category are small tracts located in mountainous areas. They supplied local domestic coal users who, at this time, no longer live there or no longer use coal as a heating fuel.

Relinquishment of such leases that have little or no importance to the western coal mining industry could save the BLM the administrative costs involved in overseeing them and could free scarce agency staff time for more important lease management responsibilities.

CONCLUDING OBSERVATIONS
AND RECOMMENDATIONS

The 99th Congress is the last to have a chance to address Section 3 before its sanctions begin to take hold on August 4, 1986. As of mid-February, 1985, two bills that either repeal or amend Section 3 have been introduced to the Senate, one by Sen. Johnston (D-La.) and one by Sen. Wallop (R.-Wyo.). More bills are expected.

Much of the data analyzed in this study suggests that the Section 3 debate to date has placed the cart before the horse. Little comprehensive analysis to identify and prioritize areas of concern that appear to hold the most merit has been undertaken. Decisions about whether or not a remedy is needed, or if some Congressional clarification of intent is desirable, should occur only after that exercise has been performed.

The principal finding in this study of Section 3 debate is that both sides are assuming that many more leases and lessees will be affected by Section 3 beginning in 1986 than is likely to be the case. While this finding does not imply the Section 3 issue is insignificant, it does suggest that Congress would be well advised to take a close look at which leases and lessees are most likely to face Section 3 before it acts. Such an examination could lead to the identification of policy alternatives appropriate to resolve particular concerns but not discussed so far. Resolution of those concerns might involve some compromise on the part of the pro-enforcement interest groups. But it might also cause an evaporation of the zeal of the pro-repeal interest groups. At worst, it would lead to a defusing of the issue.

One major area of uncertainty surrounding the implications of Section 3 involves the treatment of many types of ownership changes. If ownership changes — such as acquisition of the leaseholding company — are interpreted to restart the Section 3 clock, many companies will be relieved from facing Section 3 sanctions in 1986. If the opposite interpretation is adopted, many more lessees will face Section 3, and the potential abuse of ownership manipulations that disguise a continued control of a lease by one party will be minimized.

Clear resolution of such ownership issues should take place before Section 3 legislation is considered in earnest. The Department of Interior (DOI) has addressed some of these issues, but no comprehensive Departmental policy has been adopted as of February, 1985. In a December, 1983 letter to Senator John Warner, Chairman of the Senate Subcommittee on Energy and Mineral Resources, Interior Legislative Counsel Leonia Power states that a "100 per cent, arm's-length assignment" is an ownership change that would restart the Section 3 clock. A "draft guidance" document, issued by DOI in February, 1985 states that partial assignment of less than 100 per cent interest and lease segregations would also restart the clock for the companies involved in those transactions.

Another DOI document in January, 1985 outlines policy options for the Department with regard to implementation of Section 3. One option calls for a detailed analysis of ownership issues by the Solicitor's Office within DOI. As of the end of February, the Secretary had not made a policy decision. It is likely that Congress would benefit by having a legal interpretation of ownership issues in hand, from the Department of Interior and from other independent legal analysts if possible, before it acts on Section 3 legislation.

Based on the data collected and analyzed in this study, it appears that, overall, the arguments in favor of repeal of Section 3 are less supportable than the arguments in favor of enforcement of the provision. Such a conclusion assumes an equal weight to each argument and does not suggest specific arguments on both sides do not find support. The evidence, however, suggests that Section 3 is a less punitive requirement on pre-FCLAA lessees than suggested by those groups arguing for repeal. And its implementation will be less disruptive on the coal industry and other western mineral industries, including oil and gas, than charged. On the positive side, it appears that enforcement of Section 3 could play a role in preventing speculation, help protect areas of high environmental concern, and is likely to increase the revenue flow to state and federal treasuries.

However, some pro-enforcement arguments, such as the charge that repeal of Section 3 will provide a major financial windfall to the oil companies, do not appear well-founded. Furthermore, the tipping of the weight of the evidence in favor of the pro-enforcement arguments does not mean that implementation of Section 3, as it now reads, will not create some serious problems that could and perhaps should be avoided through amendment to the provision. For example, there is no disincentive in Section 3 against the assignment of leases to speculators before the 1986 deadline if assignment costs reach the "fire-sale" prices necessary to attract speculators. Such assignments restart the Section 3 clock and would breathe some life back into the lease speculation market, contrary to Congressional intent in 1976.

Requiring companies holding pre-FCLAA leases that have not been in production for ten years to pay advance royalties on a percentage of the coal their leases contain might prevent this activity. This would affect small speculators who do not plan to bid on other mineral leases, but do not have the financial resources to pay advance royalties for long periods of time.

Another potential problem area involves possible special hardship cases where companies have made substantial investments in mine developments, but are unlikely to meet the 1986 production deadline. Some lease or site-specific relief might be appropriate in the interests of efficient production of western coal resources. Such case-by-case analysis has not been preformed to date.

Moreover, some form of relief might be appropriate for companies within particular industries upon which the heaviest burden of Section 3 will fall. For example, companies in the steel industry hold many long-term leases that are not likely to be in production by 1986. They acquired large western coal reserves decades ago, not for their future resale value, but as part of a nationwide natural resource acquisition effort to supply long-term steelmaking needs. An assessment of the value of the industry's western reserves to its overall economic position would shed some light on the fairness of Section 3 in this special case.

As the debate heats up again, it is likely that many of the same theories and concerns will be expressed by various interest groups arguing for and against repeal or modification of Section 3 that have peppered the debate in the past. One of the few advantages of having such a debate occur so late — eight years after enactment of Section 3 and only two years before its sanctions takes effect — is that considerable information is now available with which to assess the real effects of Section 3. Some new analysis has been collected in this study in the hope that it will contribute to the separation of fact from theory in the debate and assist a constructive resolution of the controversy.

APPENDIX A: METHODOLOGY

This study was performed during the seven month period between October 1984 and April 1985. The first step was to review the published literature on the Section 3 issue to date.

The second step was to develop a computer database management system sufficiently large to record the extensive lease-specific information collected during research. The system also had to be adequately equipped with mathematical and database manipulation functions to perform the anticipated analyses. Version 1.A of the LOTUS 1-2-3 program was selected.

One, two, or three rows in the LOTUS spreadsheet were assigned as a record for one lease. Multiple rows were necessary for leases whose ownership has been or is currently split among two or more companies. The lease-specific information was of four types. The first type contained background information about each lease, such as date of issuance, size, and location. The second type contained information assessing the prospects that each lease would meet the commercial production requirement contained in Section 3. The third type contained seven columns of information about lease ownership, such as date of lease acquisition, name of lessee, and principal line of business activity. These columns were repeated for each lessee since enactment of FCLAA, including the owner at the time FCLAA became law. The fourth type contained database management codes developed during the course of the project to assist in information handling and analysis.

A list of pre-FCLAA leases and background information on each of those leases were obtained from a Lease Catalogue appended to the 1981 study of the Office of Technology Assessment entitled *An Assesssment of Development and Production Potential of Federal Coal Leases*. This information was loaded into the LOTUS format.

The OTA catalogue was also the source of information about prospects for development by 1986. The catalogue grouped contiguous leases and leases located in close proximity to each other under common ownership into blocks containing up to 19 leases. A large number of blocks contained only one lease. The OTA catalogue noted whether each lease block was included in a mine plan approved by the U.S. Office of Surface Mining or pending OSM approval, or if no mine plan had been submitted by the lessee to the OSM. The date of the OTA assessment was mid-1981.

In this study it was assumed that all leases within each block were considered to be part of a logical mining unit and would be assessed together when determining the status of their lessee to Section 3 in 1986. Thus, if commercial quantities of coal within the logical mining unit were produced by 1986, all leases in the block would be considered in production, even though the coal may have been mined from only a portion of the leases included in the unit. This interpretation appears to be consistant with federal regulations defining logical mining units and commercial quantities as they pertain to the diligent development provision contained in post-FCLAA leases.

The study used the mine plan status information contained in the OTA Catalogue as the basis for assessing prospects of achieving commercial production by 1986. It assumed that lessees of lease blocks containing approved mine plans as of mid-1981 would have no trouble meeting the 1986 deadline. It assumed that lease blocks contained in pending mine plans would face uncertain prospects of development by 1986 because the lessee still faced the obstacle of receiving regulatory agency approval. This would allow at most only five years to construct a coal mine and extract commercial quantities of coal. Lease blocks not included in a mine plan submitted to the OSM by mid-1981 were assumed to be unlikely to meet the commercial quantities obligation contained in Section 3 by 1986. One revision of OTA mine plan status was made on the basis of information collected during intervierws. Several blocks of leases in the Southwest region of Utah for which mine plans had been prepared and submitted to OSM in the 1970's were reassigned to the no-mine-plan category because the coal utilization projects they were designed to supply have been cancelled or delayed.

Lease ownership information was obtained through primary source research and consultation of secondary sources. Considerable data about lease ownership from the passage of FCLAA through the end of 1979 is contained in another OTA publication, entitled *Patterns and Trends in Federal Coal Lease Ownership: 1950 - 1980.* Additional information about lease assignments between 1976 and 1979 and new information about lease assignments between 1980 and the end of 1984 was obtained directly from primary sources. The official lease ownership records are maintained in western state Bureau of Land Management (BLM) offices where they are available for public inspection. Trips were made to BLM offices in Santa Fe, Denver, Cheyenne, and Salt Lake City during which the ownership records for every coal lease in the states of Oklahoma, New Mexico, Colorado, Utah, and Wyoming were inspected. Lease assignment data affecting the few leases in Montana and North Dakota were obtained during phone calls with a BLM official in the Billings, Montana office.

A list of all owners of federal coal leases between passage of FCLAA and the end of 1984 was complied from the ownership data. Information about corporate activities of those lessees — such as their principal business activity, the business structure, and the involvement in mergers — was obtained from a review of business and financial reference books — such as Moody's Industrial Guide — and from a review of industry trade press and the Wall Street Journal.

After lease background, development status, and ownership history information was recorded into the LOTUS spreadsheet, the record for each lease was reviewed in a two step process. First, each ownership change affecting a lease was assigned one of nine codes to reflect the category of ownership transfer involved — such as 100 per cent lease assignment or acquisition of lessee by another company. Secondly, a series of codes were assigned to each lease to reflect its overall development and ownership status with regard to the likelihood that the current lessee would face Section 3 sanctions in 1986. Three code symbols were used to assess development potential: approved mine plan, pending mine plan, and undeveloped. Similarly, the nine ownership changes were grouped into three categories according to the likelihood that they would affect lessee susceptibility to Section 3: 100 per cent lease assignment, ownership changes with uncertain implications, and no significant ownership change. Pre-FCLAA leases that have since been relinquished were deleted during the coding process. The codes greatly facilitated the lease analyses.

The data analyses were performed in large part using the various mathematical, data sorting, and data query functions contained in the LOTUS program. The 500 leases were first divided among three groups containing, respectively, high, uncertain, and low chance categories of susceptibility to Section 3. Leases were assigned to the low chance category if their codes indicated they would be in production by 1986 or if they had undergone a 100 per cent lease assignment among unaffiliated companies. Leases were assigned to the uncertain category if they had pending mine plans, but no lease assignment history or if they had no mine plans, but had experienced an ownership change with uncertain implications. Leases were assigned to the high chance category if they had no mine plans and have not been affected by any ownership change since passage of FCLAA.

The LOTUS functions could then complete the analyses contained in this study by either addressing the individual categories of leases or by addressing the entire database.

The timetable for this project was as follows:

- October — review of Section 3 literature and completion of design of the database
- November — identification of pre-FCLAA leases and recording of background data
- December to mid-January — completion of primary and secondary source research. Recording of development status and ownership histories
- Late January — completion of coding and data analyses
- February — design and completion of draft manuscript
- March — technical review and editing
- April — production and publication

APPENDIX B: BIBLIOGRAPHY

Amending The Mineral Leasing Act of 1920. Hearings before the Senate Subcommittee on Energy and Mineral Resources. Washington, DC. October 18, 1983.

Cannon, James. *Leased and Lost: A Study of Public and Indian Coal Leasing*. (New York: The Council on Economic Priorities, 1974).

Cannon, James. *Mine Control: Western Coal Leasing and Development*. (New York: The Council on Economic Priorities, 1978).

Cannon, James. *Patterns and Trends in Western Coal Lease Ownership: 1950-1980*. (Washington, DC: U.S. Office of Technology Assessment, 1981).

Federal Coal Leasing Amendments Act of 1982. Hearings before the Senate Subcommittee on Energy and Mineral Resources. Washington, DC. August 3, 1982.

National Coal Association. *An Evaluation of Selected Provisions of the Federal Leasing Amendments Act of 1976*. (Washington, DC: National Coal Association, 1983).

Sierra Club. *Old Leases - New Giveaways*. (Washington, DC: Sierra Club, 1984).

U.S. Department of Interior. *Draft Guidelines on Section 2(a)(2)(A) of the Act of February, 25, 1920, as Amended*. Federal Register. February 15, 1985.

U.S. Department of Interior. *Federal Coal Management Report, Fiscal Year 1983*. (Washington, DC. U.S. Department of Interior, 1984).

U.S. Office of Technology Assessment, *An Assessment of the Development and Production Potential of Federal Coal Leases*. (Washington, DC: U.S. Office of Technology Assessment, 1981).

COUNCIL ON ECONOMIC PRIORITIES

30 Irving Place
New York, NY 10003
212-420-1133

Join CEP Today

You Can Make a Difference!

☐ **Please enroll me as a Donor Member of CEP** and send me copies of all CEP publications — **Studies, Reports** and **Newsletters**. Membership $100. (Tax deductible.)

☐ **Please enroll me as a Sustaining Member of CEP** and send me a copy of all CEP **Reports** and **Newsletters**. Membership $50. (Tax deductible.)

☐ **Please enroll me as a Regular Member of CEP** and send me a copy of all CEP **Newsletters**. Membership $25. Students, unemployed and retired persons $15. (Tax deductible.)

☐ Please send me information on Institutional and Public Library subscriptions.

☐ Please send me a complete list of CEP publications.

Name _____

Street _____ **Apt.** _____

City _____

State _____ **Zip** _____

Phone No. (____ **)** _____

(All contributions are tax deductible.)

Council on Economic Priorities, 30 Irving Pl., New York, NY 10003

LIBRARY OF DAVIDSON COLLEGE

Books on regular loan may be checked out for **two weeks.** Books must be presented at the Circulation Desk in order to be renewed.

A fine is charged after date due.

Special books are subject to special regulations at the discretion of the library staff.